Some Animals

Some Animals

Kelli Allen

Etchings Press
Indianapolis, Indiana

Copyright© 2016 by Kelli Allen

This publication is made possible by the funding provided by the College of Arts and Sciences and the English Department at the University of Indianapolis. Special thanks to IngramSpark and to those students who judged, edited, designed, and published this chapbook: Marika Bolden and Mirna Palacio Ornelas.

UNIVERSITY *of*
INDIANAPOLIS

Published by Etchings Press
1400 E. Hanna Ave.
Indianapolis, Indiana 46227
All rights reserved

etchings.uindy.edu
www.uindy.edu/cas/english

Printed by IngramSpark
ingramspark.com

Published in the United States of America

ISBN
978-0-9903475-6-9

23 22 21 20 19 18 17 16   2 3 4
Second Printing, 2019

Table of Contents

Becoming a Woman of the Brook, Shade, and Moss	1
Market Day in Someone Else's City	2
Feeding Birds, or, rather, Some Magic	3
Folding the Invitation to Your Wedding	4
The Rooster's Daydream	5
Late Afternoon in the Tall Grass	7
Here Are Instructions for Removing the Scissors	8
Eventually, we go inside	9
Wishing Adeline and the Shooting Stars	10
If Fairy Tales in Fall	11
Eleven Years, Abandon Another Day	12
Sorrow's Argument	13
We, As Other People	14
What of Birds	15
Trebuchet	16
Aphasia	18
When He Leaves	19
How Much Tenderness, When We Consider How to Leave	20
Of Five Fears: Three of them *light*.	21
Separations for Fall, for Winter, too	22
Edging Our Wall, Untying	23
Deciding Against Marriage	24
Some Animals	25
Ghosting	26
Conversation Under Sun In Summer, Late	27
What Can We Do To Be Away From the World?	28
Hushing, like an awl through leather	29
Walking through the morning	30
Acknowledgements	33

Becoming a Woman of the Brook, Shade, and Moss

What if my body fell through bliss,
caught its last small toe on some hook
in descent? How, then, will we name
whatever is left, is aswirl, skull and clavicle
force-sculpted, at last, having roughly
fallen together to rest (wait) at the bottom
of my well, and certainly yours?

You tell me it's easy to pretend Ivan
will make room on his flaming bird's back,
when we are ready to be lifted, however restlessly,
away from woods, sea, maybe our bed suddenly
too small, knotted. You promise the feather's heat
will be worth the untying, the recognition
of this loss exchanged for riding away,
Yaga's hut distant, withering. Despite warnings,
there are only three ways to bury shame.

Before long we're asleep, mats spread over pebbles,
pillows wilted, and the beetle arrives with our keys
tucked in mandibles, tusks. The next day might
not come and no fortune hunter can reclaim
what was lost in the tucking in, folding under,
of these blankets too cool under our chins. We
will hear his wings too late and the fruit just drops,
jeweled carnage into the stream.

Market Day in Someone Else's City

Some towns are the wing bones we crush
in our hands. Every street's turn signifies
what is most hollow in the snap. Yet,
we return again as weasels emerging
from the rough barn, paws and teeth
ahold of the last map, rich cake crumbs
still falling from the scrolls' edges.

Leaving means we close the garden house
door, maybe too late, and who then will escort
the bride, her two blessed boys, and some
prince to the hall erected as center, as castle?

It's no longer enough to be the merchant
when rain refuses an audience and the procession
could stop, and there are no dances to sell,
no poppies left in our baskets, the ground dust,
too rough for this white calf, our only meal,
to lead the way ever closer, nearly home.

Feeding Birds, or, rather, Some Magic

They grow overnight, these black ducks
tucked in rain-refusing jackets, their feathers
blooming outward, once turning inward, sharp,
a pendulum humming a remembered remainder
of simple dreams—the prize for another night
spent still on water, orders for feeding forgotten.

Yours is the smallest bird, the once braced along-
side a periphery of awake and not quite. Yours
is the association of warm under the down,
nothing tainted or hardened by an afternoon
guessing which of your wings will prove
greenest when the sun agrees to provide
just enough light to make all of this more,
never less, than water from your dream to mine.

Folding the Invitation to Your Wedding

There is a plow waiting near my broken flashlight. Both
promise a variation of warmth, perhaps warmth though
what I can expect to carry by pushing under, giving root,
perhaps by some illumination not yet anchored enough
for closeness here, this page asking for response, for
a bond of sorts. What can I ask of you? You, who lets a foot
stay tucked under warm sand, hands in pockets, coarse
hair falling ever over one cheek or the other? The curve
of you a fleshy question mark near such open waters.

Why this snuggle into writing when shown the useless
tool and the cylinder all broken plastic and glass? Objects
meant to signify desire for reciprocity become, instead,
talismans for clumsy loss, for wanting more, always more,
than I am ready to let bare in the dirt. It's pale, when it touches
my skin, this god-hand of distance, this god-touch of absence.

The Rooster's Daydream

My father was a swelling over
the soft brown hen, his beak punctuating
her neck, irrigating her dreams
of chicks drying their fluff near rocks
pebbling the curve around her stream.

Their bodies moved in an unfurling, both
trying not to be harsh with the other
in this sun, in the open dirt where fences
dotted a periphery. Theirs was a blooming,
however sudden, warped by cats narrowing
eyes, snakes uncoiling in the heat and noise.

His adoration was quick in the way
that fingers are fast when dipping
into a honeycomb, exploring the beehive
just long enough to gather sweetness
in secret. When the trees ripen,
I remember first the gathering of sound,
ghosted couplings and feathers
everywhere under their rough claws.

When the petals fall waxy in pools,
I imagine my father retrieving
his posture, letting the hen, my mother, curl away
from his wing and neither he nor she
can possibly notice the waiting ax, its nest
a richly ringed post, old-berry red, alert.

My body is the population left
in this dreaming. My breast a constellation
of hollow quill and down resting on one
blossom after another, their pink hearts tiny
boats carrying me as an eyelet snapping,
finally, against perfect silver metal. My head
bent on the way to receiving my crown.

Late Afternoon in Tall Grass

Mice rest their knees against softening dirt
and we turn further away from the east.

When I sat upon my horse, waiting
for you to come outside, I saw the henhouse shades
move twice with the breeze we talked about all morning—
how it forces our halls to smell like cinnamon until night.

There are exhausted wrens dotting the ground near these hooves.
I have not seen a grub for miles. One thin-breasted bird
shifts her leg and everything near-golden tufts into the air, a circus.

We used to rush around, with these bodies set tight as jaws
and missed the dandelion boats skimming our legs as we ran,
hurried for the shore that somehow never moved as far away
from our sobriety as we were from its drunken lap and swirl over sand.

When you come, there might still be stones in my pocket, bread
packed neatly in the saddle, a balance cast while pretending
the path to some castle must be here, marked by the angleworms
drying flat near old rainwater in our field.

Here Are Instructions for Removing the Scissors

Take the bribe offered and just plunge your entire
arm, full past the twist of elbow, into the cool muck.

Take this moment as an opening of determined appetite—
the blades are yours once pulled into the grass. Yours.

Take whatever weird laughter you hear behind your shoulder
as balm, a resolve for how far you can open, can exhale, and can search.

Take slippery weeds, darkening further down, lightening as they snake
up your wrist into the fading day, as a message—everything feeds, waits.

Take dense mud around your fingers and pull tightly the looped handle
as you dislodge the entirety of silver from this reeking, shallow pond.

Take every opportunity to own and wield the weapons for cutting, as everything begs, at some sharp moment, to be severed, to be made sweetly clean.

Eventually, we go inside.

You stack the stones as rabbits
mounted one atop the other, this field
in blue light, moss peppered with heather,
sometimes wild ferns, licking behind
your ankles as you work.

When we stepped into this opening, flanked
by mirroring puddles, and the sand hill
maze sat far behind, we knew
the thickest part of finding our way
back would come long after
a conversation, punctuated as it would be
with silences, and shuffling our feet
in rough, complicated circles—you
building pillars instead of gathering my fingers
in yours, reassuring, communing, and me,
watching your hands fill only with stones.

Even after I let my sweater fall open, then drop
to whorl into an angora pool in the thistle-pocked
clover against your boot, you would not stop
building, higher and more delicately balanced,
with those rocks, filigreed against this darkening sky.
> I breathed *touch me* and the words met only air,
> the spell cast becoming little other than pennies
> left on the path, the one we marked, some time
> ago, in chalked letters, as *this way, home.*

Wishing Adeline and the Shooting Stars

Sometimes, the book is a swan. Moments will pass and pages will curl up and away and the lines are lost for an hour as words find succor in a pond close to our window. This is not a story about goodbye. We may not know how to lurch from this world into the next, but we understand the impulse to keep our softest feathers just above water, our tails flinching toward something like sky, something like sheets billowing above us. I have neglected to tell you that not once in my whole life have I left the slipper on the stairs. Perhaps this is a story about leaving, but the kind that you and I never do, our attention as rabbits nuzzling the leash.

I made a wish, which is risky and makes you captive to the telling, but when the dandelion pop decided to lose every seed at once, what choice did I have? So many limbs are invisible in their last blossomings, even when scattering after my own pinkish tongue begs the field, the bigger flower, to wait, wait.

When we claim it, the book comes home and the story is finally about closing tight, a wishing won. I am steadfast, unruly in my quiet, and my eyes shut twice when I remember you, too, taste the busy stems as they fall beneath us.

If Fairy Tales in Fall

It isn't so much that the leaves are dizzy
as it is they are lodged in confusion, the same
variety that persuades us to jump when the waters
are on the rise. We say, "look" as our feet reappear
after tumbling over our shoulders on the way
down, we tremble and spill over. The repair work
is universal as the rake scratches our sides.

I contain so much thinning, yet lushness is my fresco
when I stop at the bottom of the well, climb back
into the bucket and yell up "It matters! It matters!" until
only the rope tail hangs near the stone rim. Nothing
whorls up in a shock the way a name does, when its ours,
all peacock and hiss, all vowel and cinnamon.

You have been told how to cut back the trestle, to light
the lamp and fold your hands. This way, we are advocates
together for a splayed phrase and retelling. The only stories
we can give back are ones considerate of the moss digesting the ledge.

Eleven Years, Abandon Another Day

You still push the envelopes through the iron rails
onto grass seldom cut, leaving the bright papers to wait
tiny and bird-light, for a possible wind to carry them closer
to her front door. It is disaster to push against the cold
and watch you. Your gesture is a song, and my stale brow
is the bag of mice our father threw down the well, punctuating
our final summer in his home with something easier for him
to say than *forget it all*.

She left her own note, a simple paragraph framed
by pink and yellow tea roses. I read the words to you
because our father hunched into his own curl of disbelief
and remained round in some residue of voice that leaned
more into silence than rough cries, which we heard only once,
at night. Somehow this matters in the way that cats carry
the nearly dead to their kittens as an offering, yes, and a command.

We listen on the way back to my house, where I teach you again
how not to vanish, for bells from her church to ring the hour,
exactly seven tones, all even. This has become home despite
his filling with smoke, hers with simple, dark corners, yours,
always tethered, twin orphans in a terminal made of sand, to mine.

Sorrow's Argument

On the day before we learn to distrust it, grief is welcome.
It soaks us with heavy wet gratitude in being able to feel
anything at all. We take grief down into our throats and hold
it thick just above our bellies. The not quite fullness reminds us
of the way back up and through, past our lips, is breath and, eventually,
song. There are four words for this: *waiting, resistance, sigh, alchemy*.

The day it arrives fully announced and inconsiderate of our day-
dreams, we pretend its calls are to others and leave the door
soundly shut. Grief, when eaten too quickly, burns the stomach
bright with holes meant for falling through, inside out, and no well
equals the pitch-and-pull we glimpse only after we tumble over
the edge. There are four words for this: *bags, root, turning, final.*

In the days after, grief is christened soft sorrow, seeming as white
snow piling all afternoon while children sleep. Sorrow is a mysterious
thief taking wasps carrying our grief into an unknown, distant summer.
We should be thankful and blink, laugh. They are neighbors, grief and
   sorrow,
as their trickery is our acceptance of blindness, our desire for something
sweet. There are four words for this: *attachment, underbelly, heft, charity.*

We, As Other People

We've been very happy in the small open area
we named *alter*. When we lay down,
it is a fragile offering, ellipses of arms,
galaxies of fox-light hairs, moving,
a division between tremble and bristle.

This is what other people do in the dark.

Sometimes, they let light in and the scene
shifts. There are occasions for fire,
kindling as mirror, candles, too, for them—
bodies without growing dis-ease, anchored
to luck, devouring wishless time. Others
are fragrant with each other, bits
of raspberries wait on their tongues.

Not us. Ours is the thumbtack mapping
where in my body the image darkens, where
under inverted triangles of breast meeting breast
the roundness grows cloudy. We live, devour
by recent scans, which we will continue
to hang here, this museum of us, until alter
becomes shrine, becomes definition for a new
lover. Here were other people, who were *us*, before you.

What of Birds?

We credit the feather's shape for their momentum, but our own battered skin
flutters unseen, toward errors of unknowing. We are spoons turned against
capturing wetness, slick curves refusing to bow inward. To communicate
softness in avigation, we must forget impulses tentative, and just, as they
do, these birds, dive behind currents. This is saying *hid*; this is saying *it's too
much to care*. When I ask you if there has been a difference in one thousand
years of eyes trained upward, forced through certain jealously, into awe,
I expect an answer laced through with an erudition enough to make me
properly jealous. It is too easy to accept the son overtaking the father, a breeze
breathing the young higher, the aged remaining an immobile windmill by the
barn. This is my response to your response, leaving us no closer to reprieve.
We might never know how to explain what hurts us as we travel
through one alliance after another, no closer to our own waxless flight.

Trebuchet

It is easy to hide
one father inside
of another, as you have,
my father, so many of you
tucked tight, as nesting
dolls without seams.
As the painted wooden set
you brought back to me
from Holland, each miniature face
smaller than the one before.

Those dolls made sense,
in their nestling logic, though
sense is a weak gray raven
to a small girl.

Now, when you cannot speak
through any of your mouths
and I have learned to lean
against your shoulder
as you lean into mine
for the first time, the dolls
will no longer open. Whatever passes
for secret belongs to them, paint
cracked only slightly, seams tight, sticking.

I think of lambs, sometimes
covered in thick zebra's stripes,
embossed to the touch,
and their new bodies
become one of you.

Aphasia

You know the way it broke
loose, the brick, from inside
our second house, a moment before
we decided on breakfast. You said
> *I put both hands in the space
> where the mortar took rot, both hands. Still
> the clay won't take, I cannot force a brick.*

Today is like that, with me watching your thick fingers

paused as cups in the air, sensing the way your hands gathered
the red chips and dust from our floor. Now, both hands
wait for something else to fall into them. It isn't just
your face, wet from internal rain, telling me to surrender.

When I said *Dad* and you could not turn to meet my voice,
when only those hands lifted out and up, palms too dry,
could I remember that none of us live in a room, that our walls,
no matter how they pinch and pioneer our lessons, contain
so little of what we often meant to say. Really say.

When He Leaves

The stamp on the back of her hand has faded
the same way a favorite tree stump stays
against some remembrance of childhood
we no longer attempt to name.

When the ink was fresh, it was a simple possibility
of a bluish shark, lines afuzz, teeth obscured,
the cartoon bubbliness of a shape made to exorcise
fear, to produce momentary joy. For her,
the image marked time spent with her father
after one morning chasing mottled geese, grey
as January, through the only park she knew
this well. She asked for balloons, a bouquet to affirm
light, and she was gifted both the blossoms of thin color
and a single pale stamp from a vendor charmed
into stooping low and adoring her pale, pale skin.

So, it tastes like something, this moment before
I let the words leave my mouth. Not quite
bitter, or pungent the way she and I both love
dark olives, pits intact, hard reminders. No,
it tastes like softness, as when bread goes beyond
staleness into the waiting for greens and acceptance
of being covered, lost completely, transformed.

How Much Tenderness, When We Consider How To Leave

We said it would be dry by morning, and so left
your name, wet, on the doorframe. It was simple,
to leave this bodily inked artifact of you as something
of a warning against entrance: Come in, please, but know
everything died within and left signatures without.

The burial was more complicated. We sat you between us
on the long bench just inside the funeral parlor, admiring
the latticework of brass and wood, which served as crown
molding in this small room. I whispered, *just like Alice
in the Queen's hall*, and waited, looking down at the cylinder
wherein you, something of you, rested all dust and what must seem
like so many broken black sand shells to the fire keeper
who placed you first in the flames, and then, here, in this silver
capsule. I say *between us*, but there was really only me, if we count
presence as more than breath and completely still hands in a lap.

Interment is a misleading word. We can never blanket enough dirt
to hide what is missing. If I could have cut my heart into enough
pieces to feed you, I would have done so at least twice. Now,
I take a photograph of the earth being piled over this ringed swatch
of indentation in the ground. The image will hang loose, near
your name dried blackish against wood, an artifact to mark
every time I will pretend to knock, enter anyway, the one space
never really my home. Someone else offers the morning prayer.

OF FIVE FEARS: THREE OF THEM *LIGHT.*

It refuses to fall from the sky, bloated
arrogance of brightness, a round bird

preening mid-air, whether we watch, or not.
And I came here to watch, that much
is clearly almost certain.

Nothing moves with that kind of light
forcing reflections where there should be
only darkening shadows. I am already angry

to have written *shadows, light, darkening.* Anger
is a shunt difficult to remove, tissues
growing around, forming something
of a structure, again, bulked against

light. Letting it in, this light, again
seeing the word here, means imagining

the bird has won over actually allowing
the self to see a wing, feel
a ripped feather, watch the feeding.

Separations for Fall, for Winter, too

What's unlikely is this rain. Even
the sparrows are agitated
and waiting. But I am contacting
you, not for some contract to be signed,
finally. Rather, I want us to hurry
across and ripen the letters for evidence
of closing. We have lodged
complaints before and each skims
the pond quick, a rehearsal we perform
in fog. What is likely is assumed distance.

We are not the same small animals
curled against blurred margins
and dropped pebbles. Our hands let
go their thefts months ago. I can hardly
remember accumulations. This is
to convey regret, maybe desire,
too, as my tongue waits, turtle-
shelled in the mouth.

Edging Our Wall, Untying

There is pressure between my hand and the reaching. We ask
longing to become a city for us, but what do we say
when the windows blow inward instead of out
and the streets flood again and again? If I am the length
of this want, and you are the width of some container
as we build up and out, how can we hope to plant grass
near the temple which will be, of course, the center of it all?

I have a bag attached to one wrist and blueprints tight
in a scroll attached to the other. Leaving either on the road
means that we are finished. There are tourists afoot, and we
are drenched in something like snow. This may be a diagnosis
I am offering. It may be a solution for the obvious anxiety
of bending our faces down, teeth spaced
to let the wind come in, come in.

Deciding Against Marriage

It is a jeweled evening and everything
everywhere is mechanical bliss. We have
forgotten migration, and these cogs
stand in for feathered movements.

The oils are as rich as ever, even
though they coat copper and water
wicks its way off other wings.

Ours is an automated afterglow. The release
comes in the rewind, the start-again of wheels
crafted in what might have been our back-
yard, had we waded deep enough in the muck to ask.

SOME ANIMALS

There is a patterned crosshatch in the armor
and no amount of rubbing lessens its impact.

Distraction is the handmaiden of complacency,
or some such thing. I am waiting for a trick

of light to let me shout "what a kingdom!" and go away,
heels clicking *onetwo onetwo* on the marble leading out.

I want this experience to be unpolluted. I want the end
to be a trajectory of my own making. Nothing upsets

contentment quicker than intentionally disturbed metal.
Where is the glimmer, the Alexandrian hangman of glory

cast against steel? Sometimes the only salvation
is in the heron that swoops down from a skylight

we did not even notice to spread wing and waters
over the arch of a shield, of a blade.

Ghosting

Who points the way, holds out a gloved hand
with a single, simple sign stating *This way*?
What book officially begs us to give attention
to a list of rules which includes *You may only ask
one question of the steward?* What if the answer
to both queries has been carved in shallow print
into soapstone ever nearing the shoreline's
inevitable lick and curl? We should admit
there is sense in answers near wetness. Swallowing
is its own sign—a reflex won at birth, repeated
with every phrase, every taken pleasure.

I think of this as ghosting. What came before
certainly does not wish for us to forget
and so offers a seeding of questions, which we embrace
without intention, and this I call, not paranoia,
rather knowing-lust. That radiance we suspect
has been threaded into our every lysosome, namelessly,
unearned, ours as a right of carrying cells upon
cells until we think we might be whole, is never
really new and so we keep vigil for signifiers.

Conversation Under Sun In Summer, Late

The ear has its own mood, wants
to succeed, wants to know
more than the curve and bell
of itself. The ear finds water rushing,
confesses mistakes easily, begs
to be cupped against dampness,
against translations in the upper register.

We speculate that there is a noble problem
when the ear resists our distinctions, lumps
us together in a singular song, leaves us
to our own arguments, even though our knees touch
once and my fingers find again, too quick, your shoulder.
We are over-flown with sounds marked less
by contrast than by interference. I hear your lips
against the cup and wonder where...when.

Perhaps the teacher has taught her student
to listen through the mouth. There is safety
in the simple shape of each vowel. Leave
the ear to a shade of enthusiastic ripeness
gathered when the head is pushed closely, tilted
to catch a dress' hem sighing up from a damp thigh.

We are nearing the door to the room where my ear
presses close to the mat used sometimes for prayer,
sometimes just for kneeling.

What Can We Do To Be Away From the World?

We think we might go north, the way the stamen puffs firm
against the mid-day breeze. It's an old silence that gives us pause,
makes us bend our spines back into the pillows, you reaching
up to push the window a crack higher, the length of your arm
dangerous in its pale, in my desire to trace the elbow's bend
once with my tongue tipped hard.

The way you worry is an easy country compared to just how much
I keep hidden, the weight of hiding becoming its own
language when we meet, later in the day, the week, as strangers.

Those maps for whatever comes in the pretending night
when you have climbed above me, slow pushing, being taken
inward, are peeling quickly from the brick and I catch your eye,
just once, widening as you recognize that when paper meets ground,
we will have nothing left to plan, to explain, to wish.

Hushing, like an awl through leather

First, the body is bent. And we
barely speak into the maw
of the potbellied stove
as we feed logs tighter
into such fullness.

Someone I knew once
hummed each movement
from that song you love
and now, while you arch
your back into stretch, bones
a whimper through this too cool night,
I want nothing more
than to slither soft behind
and collect your wrists
with my tongue while you tell me
what it is to crave a proper scratch
behind hairy ears. We might meet
again, later

in leanings against that old church,
its bell weighted by your stories, not mine,
and I will tell you, then, ash still
under my boot, why I asked you
to come inside.

Walking through the morning

You may have slept all night and we walk
together past the horses, who are out early
on this Sunday and their necks bending
down becomes the prologue for this: I saw you carry
your boots, cradle them like oysters plucked too soon
from cool brine. The mud, you told me later, came
from the river, undersides of oak and willow pocking
leather. It does not matter where you decide to rest
the objects you value. It matters even less
how such labor is as perishable as the apple
rolling by your bare feet.

The mares don't see us as we see ourselves, as I
look at you and say "Dear one. Never mind.
You were already come and gone. I made the bed
up tight. The lights are on. They're still on."

Acknowledgments

"When He Leaves" appeared in *2 Bridges Review*.

"Aphasia" and "How Much Tenderness" appeared in *Linden Avenue*.

"Of Five Fears, three of them *light.*" appeared in *Architrave*.

"Ghosting" appeared in *The Boiler Journal*.

"Sorrow's Argument" and "What of Birds" appeared in *TAB*.

"Eleven Years" appeared in *Abridged*.

"We as Other People" appeared in *Gravel*.

"If Fairy Tales in Fall" appeared in *Modern Poetry Quarterly Review*.

"Edging Our Wall, Untying," "Deciding Against Marriage," "Some Animals," "Separations for Fall, for Winter, too," and "Folding the Invitation to Your Wedding" all appeared in *The Inflectionist Review* (featured Distinguished Poet section).

"Here Are Instructions for Removing the Scissors" appeared in *East Bay Review*.

COLOPHON

Cover text and poem titles set in Avenir.
Body text set in EB Garamond.

Kelli Allen's work has appeared in numerous journals and anthologies in the US and internationally. She is a four-time Pushcart Prize nominee and has won awards for her poetry, prose, and scholarly work. She served as Managing Editor of *Natural Bridge* and holds an MFA from the University of Missouri St. Louis. She is the director of the *River Styx* Hungry Young Poets Series and founded the Graduate Writers Reading Series for UMSL. She is currently a Professor of Humanities and Creative Writing at Lindenwood University. Allen is the author of two chapbooks and numerous scholarly articles. Her full-length poetry collection, *Otherwise, Soft White Ash,* arrived from John Gosslee Books in 2012 and was nominated for the Pulitzer Prize.

www.kelli-allen.com

Etchings Press

Etchings Press is a student-run publisher at the University of Indianapolis. Each year, student editors choose the Whirling Prize, a post-publication award, in the fall and coordinate a publication contest for one poetry chapbook, one prose chapbook, and one novella in the spring. For more information, please visit etchings.uindy.edu.

Previous winners and publications

Poetry
2019: *As Lovers Always Do* by Marne Wilson
2018: *In the Herald of Improbable Misfortunes* by Robert Campbell
2017: *Uncle Harold's Maxwell House Haggadah* by Danny Caine
2016: *Some Animals* by Kelli Allen
2015: *Velocity of Slugs* by Joey Connelly
2014: *Action at a Distance* by Christopher Petruccelli

Prose
2019: *Dissenting Opinion from the Committee for the Beatitudes* by Marc J. Sheehan (fiction)
2018: *The Forsaken* by Chad V. Broughman (fiction)
2017: *Unravelings* by Sarah Cheshire (memoir)
2016: *Pathetic* by Shannon McLeod (essays)
2015: *Ologies* by Chelsea Biondolillo (essays)
2014: *Static: Stories* by Frederick Pelzer (fiction)

Novella
2019: *Savonne, Not Vonny* by Robin Lee Lovelace
2018: *Edge of the Known Bus Line* by James R. Gapinski
2017: *The Denialist's Almanac of American Plague and Pestilence* by Christopher Mohar
2016: *Followers* by Adam Fleming Petty